ANDROCLES AND THE LION

GETTING READY FOR YOUR PLAY

Characters:
Soldier #1, Soldier #2, Soldier #3,
Soldier #4, Androcles, Lion, Nero,
nobles, ladies, courtiers

Props:
rock/throne, 4 swords, 4 shields,
chairs, violin,
"triumphal" marching music

Suggestions:
1. Swords and shields can be made from cardboard.
2. Chairs for nobles and ladies can be placed in a straight line with backs toward audience. On the back of each chair hang butcher paper with foliage painted for scenery. When the scene changes to the arena, have courtiers turn chairs and place in semicircle around throne for ladies and nobles to sit on.
3. Lion can be given full costume or paint whiskers on face and use a striped helmet with lion ears.
4. A stool may be used as the rock/throne.

CAST

Character:	Actor/Actress:
Soldier #1	_____
Soldier #2	_____
Soldier #3	_____
Soldier #4	_____
Androcles	_____
Lion	_____
Nero	_____
Nobles	_____
	_____
	_____
	_____
Ladies	_____
	_____
	_____
	_____
Courtiers	_____
	_____
	_____
	_____

ANDROCLES AND THE LION

(Scene takes place in the woods outside of Rome in 54 A.D. The rock is placed SC. Two soldiers with swords and shields enter DSR and look around—poking here and there with their swords.)

Soldier #1: I know I saw him enter this part of the woods!

Soldier #2: He can't go far on foot!

Soldier #1: *(crossing USL)* You're right. He won't last long hiding in these woods. Last week a lion was killed less than two kilometers from here!

Soldier #2: *(crossing DSR)* Why would a slave want to escape from his master?

Soldier #1: *(crossing DSC)* Would you want to be a slave? Would you want to be owned—like a dog—with a collar around your neck?

Soldier #2: *(crossing DSC)* No! I'm lucky I'm a Roman! Free to go and do as I please. *(puts down sword and shield and sits on rock SC)*

Soldier #1: *(puts foot on rock)* That's fate! You were lucky to be born in Rome and Androcles, the slave, was unlucky to be born in a country Rome conquered.

Soldier #2: I'll say he's unlucky! When they capture Androcles, he will be forced to fight the lions at the arena, and... *(A noise is heard from off stage left. Both soldiers jump up in alarm!)*

Soldier #1: *(pointing USL)* The noise came from there!

Soldier #2: *(picks up sword and shield)* Come on, let's get him! *(both run off stage left)*

Androcles: *(running on from DSL)* I have to stop! I'm exhausted! I can't run anymore! *(sits on rock, breathing deeply)* I'll sit on this rock and rest. *(a noise from offstage right)* More soldiers? I have to escape! *(tries to rise, but falls back down)* I can't move. I'm exhausted!

Lion: *(enters DSR, limping)* Rrow—rrrowww—rrroooowww!

Androcles: *(frightened)* How much worse can life get? *(gestures left)* Soldiers to the left about to capture me... *(gestures right)* and a lion to the right about to eat me! *(hides behind rock)*

Lion: *(limping across stage)* R-r-o-o-o-w-w-w! *(sits DSL)* I am in pain! Help!

Androcles: *(peeking over rock)* A lion that talks? I must be dreaming!

Lion: No. You think you hear words, but we are communicating mentally. Help me!

Androcles: *(standing)* This is crazy! I'm exhausted and out of my mind!

Lion: I need your help!

Androcles: *I* can help *you*?

Lion: Yes! *(holds up paw)* I have a thorn in my paw! The humans are chasing me with their dogs and I can run no farther.

Androcles: We've got a lot in common! My exact story! *(starts toward lion)* Of course I'll help you! *(stops)* What am I doing? A lion! I'll be eaten alive!

Lion: Trust me! Why would I eat you? I need you to help me!

Androcles: *(inches toward lion)* Really?

Lion: *Really*! With you I'll be tame.

Androcles: *(touches lion's paw)* A tame, man-eating lion!

Lion: R-r-r-r-ooooooo-w-w-w-w-w!

Androcles: *(jumps back)* Why did you do that?

Lion: It hurts! A thorn in the paw hurts!

Androcles: Of course. *(gingerly takes paw and pulls out thorn)* There!

Lion: *(holds paw and smiles)* Relief! *(looks at Androcles)* You know, for a human you're OK. What's your name?

Androcles: Androcles.

Lion: Call me "Lee." That's short for Leo. Why are you here in the woods?

Androcles: I'm a slave. I'm running to freedom.

Lion: I figured as much. *(dogs bark off SL)* Uh oh, the dogs! This is it, pal! *(runs off DSR)*

Androcles: *(calling after him)* Run, Lee! Run for your life! *(turns and runs DSL bumping into soldiers running in SL)*

Soldier #1: Halt, slave! *(points sword at Androcles)* Who were you calling after?

(Androcles turns and runs USR as a soldier intercepts him.)

Soldier #2: (*sword raised*) Halt, in the name of the Emperor!

(*Androcles turns and runs DSR as Soldier #3 runs in to stop him.*)

Soldier #3: (*draws sword*) Your time has come!

(*Androcles turns and starts to run USL, but right then a soldier enters USL.*)

Soldier #4: (*sword drawn and slowly walking toward Androcles*) Consider yourself captured!

(*Androcles turns frantically to all exits, but soldiers slowly walk toward him and pen him in.*)

Androlces: (*dropping to his knees*) You've got me! I give up!

Soldier #1: On your feet, slave!

Androcles: Where are you taking me?

Soldier #2: Rome.

Androcles: (*suspicious*) Why Rome?

Soldier #3: Nero, our fiddling Emperor, wants to invite you to a show at the arena. (*Soldiers laugh together.*)

Androcles: The arena!! Where men fight lions bare-handed?

Soldier #4: Exactly! And you'll be the main attraction! (*pokes Androcles*) March!

(*All exit SR marching as "triumphal" music starts. Roman courtiers enter SL, pick up rock and carry it USC, inverting it to become a throne. Enter the Emperor SL followed by Roman nobles and ladies. They all circle the stage parading to the music. The Emperor sits on the throne and the others sit on either side of him, making a semicircle. Enter Androcles surrounded by the four soldiers. They stop in front of the Emperor.*)

(*Music stops.*)

Soldier #1: Your Highness, here is Androcles, the captured slave.

Nero: (*rises and walks around Androcles, inspecting him*) A puny slave, to be sure!

(*A lion roars loudly from SL.*)

Androcles: (*knees shaking*) That lion sounds hungry!

Nero: Hasn't been fed in two days! (*looks at Androcles, who sinks as two soldiers hold him up*) Oh, my. I fear this is going to be a short performance.

Androcles: Maybe we could cancel!

Nero: I like a good show—don't disappoint me! (*walks to throne and sits*) Or I'll find something worse for you to battle!

Androcles: (*shaking*) What could be worse??!! (*closes eyes*)

Noble: (*calling off SL*) Let loose the lion!

Lion: (*runs on stage and roars*) R-R-RRR O-O-OOOO W-W-www

(*Soldiers scatter in fright as lion and Androcles lock in a wrestling hold—twisting and turning, grunting and roaring. Nobles and ladies politely clap and lightly cheer "bravo."*)

Androcles: (*looks at face of lion*) Lee!

Lion: (*looks at face of Androcles*) Androcles!

Androcles: I can't strangle you!

Lion: I can't tear you to shreds!

Androcles: (*whispers, still locked in hold*) What'll we do? The Emperor wants a show!

Lion: (*whispering*) Well, let's give him one. Just clap your hands and watch!

(*Androcles jumps aside and claps hands. Lion runs in a circle, jumps up and hits his heels together twice, then sits and begs. Audience sits with their mouths open, stunned.*)

Nero: Amazing!

(*Androcles claps his hands again and lion does a somersault, then leaps up in the air.*)

Nero: (*rising*) Incredible!

Androcles: (*looking up and seeing he is impressing noble audience*) And now, for a final trick! Lee,. . .ah, Leo the Lion will perform a gravity-defying aerial trick. (*Androcles claps hands and lion jumps up, does a cartwheel and ends standing on one foot in a graceful pose.*)

Everyone: (*rising and cheering*) Bravo! Cheers! Great! Wonderful!

(*Androcles and the lion take deep bows to the audience—then bow to each other—then bow again to nobles and ladies.*)

Nero: (*raises hand*) Bring the prisoners forward!

(*Soldiers run on and escort Androcles and lion to Emperor.*)

Nero: Never have these arena walls encompassed such a performance. You are both given your freedom,. . .(*everyone cheers*) but with one condition! You, Androcles, will produce all future shows here at the arena—starring you and Leo, of course!

(*Androcles and lion play hard-to-get and consult each other in whispers. Nero and nobles lean forward in anticipation.*)

Androcles: Agreed! (*everyone cheers*) But there is one condition: All slaves must be freed to become actors and all captured lions will be fed and given a warm bed at the new Lion Forest Preserve.

Nero: Agreed! (*everyone cheers*) One small thing, (*crosses to Androcles and puts his arm around his shoulder*) Andy! (*pulls violin out from under toga*) I play a mean fiddle. Do you think you could find a place for me in your next show? (*Nero starts to fiddle. Lion crosses eyes and Androcles winces as everyone tiptoes off stage, fingers stuck in ears. Nero looks around, finds himself alone, bows, looks embarrassed, and runs off. Everyone runs back on and bows.*)

THE END

ANDROCLES AND THE LION

PRODUCTION NOTES

Use this sheet to keep personal notes about any aspect of your production: costumes, characters, stage directions, props, rehearsals, performances, evaluations, etc.

THE GOLD MEDALS

GETTING READY FOR YOUR PLAY

Characters:
Samaranch, IOC Member #1,
IOC Member #2, IOC Member #3,
IOC Member #4, Secretary, Wheeler,
Mother, Jim, School Official,
Pop Warner, Jesse, George,
voice offstage, AAU President
Avery Brundage.

Props:
table, namecard, 7 chairs, paper, pencils, steno pad, apron, 2 hats, press card, football helmet, football, 2 pairs of track shoes, gunfire sound effect, cheering crowd sound effects, 2 gold medals with ribbons, notebook, paper ballots

Suggestions:
1. Try to get a football helmet in the style of the early 1900's.
2. Jim can be wearing a football jersey.
3. Try to get a telephone of the 1920's. If you can't, reporter can reach OFF SL for the phone and when finished, hand it back to someone offstage.
4. Ballots can state, "When Jim Thorpe's name was removed from the Olympic record book, runners-up were made champions and given his medals—Ferdinand Bie of Norway (Pentathlon) and Hugo Wieslander of Sweden (Decathlon). Should Jim Thorpe's name be written in the book as co-champion with each of these men, or should their names be removed, their medals returned, and Jim Thorpe be made full Champion? Please vote."
(If this is too much to print on ballots, Samaranch can make this statement as he distributes the ballots.)

CAST

Character:	Actor/Actress
Samaranch	_____
IOC Member #1	_____
IOC Member #2	_____
IOC Member #3	_____
IOC Member #4	_____
Secretary	_____
Wheeler	_____
Mother	_____
Jim	_____
School Official	_____
Pop Warner	_____
Jesse	_____
George	_____
Voice offstage	_____
Avery Brundage	_____

THE GOLD MEDALS

(Scene takes place at a meeting of the International Olympic Committee. The year is 1982. The President of the IOC, Juan Antonio Samaranch, is seated at a table USC. His name is on a large card on the table in front of him. Four members of the IOC are also seated at the table, two on either side of the President. All members have papers to refer to. A secretary sits at the end of the table SR and writes notes on a steno pad. There are two empty chairs SL at the end of the table. Members are talking to each other.)

Samaranch: Will the committee please come to order! We are reviewing the case of Jim Thorpe, USA, Gold Medalist in the 1912 Olympics in Stockholm.

IOC Member #1: *(referring to paper)* Yes, he placed "gold" in the Pentathlon...

IOC Member #2: *(interrupting)* Which in those days was the long jump, javelin, 200 meters, discus, and 300 meters.

IOC Member #3: *(reading paper)* And the Decathlon, which is the same as today...

IOC Member #4: *(interrupting)* the shot put, long jump, high jump, javelin throw, discus throw, 110-meter hurdles, pole vault, and the 100, 400, and 1500-meter runs.

Samaranch: Yes. As you know, he was stripped of his gold medals and his name was stricken from the Olympic records. We are urged by Mr. Robert Wheeler, the well-known historian, to consider reversing that decision made over 50 years ago. But I'll let Mr. Wheeler tell the story. *(to secretary)* Miss Buckley, please ask Mr. Wheeler to come in.

Secretary: *(rises and crosses SR)* Mr. Wheeler.

Wheeler: *(enters SR and crosses to shake hands with Samaranch)* Thank you for reviewing this case.

Samaranch: *(motions to chair SL)* Please explain Jim Thorpe's background to the members.

Wheeler: Before I begin, let me say that this man was declared "best athlete of the first half of the century" by an Associated Press poll of sports writers. And when the King of Sweden placed the gold medals around Thorpe's neck at the 1912 Olympics, he said, "Sir, you are the greatest athlete in the world." *(to committee)* This, my friends, is still true! But let me start from the beginning. *(motions DSC)* Picture a small cabin on an Indian reservation in Oklahoma. Jim's mother is preparing supper...

More Short Plays for the Classroom—Intermediate No. 2479

(Enter mother from SL. She is wearing an apron and pantomimes setting the table, then goes DSR to call for Jim.)

Mother: *(calls off SR)* Jim! Jim, come in and get ready for supper.

Jim: *(enters DSR)* Boy, am I hungry!

Mother: You're filthy! What have you been doing?

Jim: Breaking the new colt! *(brings empty chair DSC and then pantomimes while talking)* First you sneak up on the horse, *(sneaks up to chair)* lasso him *(throws imaginary rope)*, hold him with the rope 'cause he's buckin' and kickin'! Then when he starts to tire you *leap (straddles chair)* on his back, hang on, and then . . .

Mother: *(laughing)* I know. I've seen you do it a hundred times. It's a wonder you don't break every bone in your body when you get thrown off!

Jim: Oh, it doesn't hurt! Besides, I'm getting stronger—I don't get bucked off so often any more!

Mother: Your grandfather would be proud of you. You are certainly living up to your Indian heritage.

Jim: I *am* proud to be an Indian!

(knock at door off SR)

Mother: *(calling off SR)* Come in!

School Official: *(taking off hat)* Mrs. Thorpe?

Mother: Yes.

School Official: I represent Carlisle Indian School in Pennsylvania.

Jim: I've heard of Carlisle. Pop Warner is football coach there!

School Official: That's right. My job is to scout all the Indian Reservations around the United States looking for athletes. Jim, I think you're a natural! We'd be pleased to have you as a student at Carlisle.

Mother: But Pennsylvania is so far away!

School Official: *(to Mother)* I think I can convince you that this would be a great opportunity for Jim. I'd like to tell you all about Carlisle. Why don't we go out on the porch and talk it over? I have a feeling that your answer will be "yes."

(All exit DSR.)

Wheeler: *(to committee)* And Jim did say, "yes." In 1906, at Carlisle, Glen "Pop" Warner immediately saw his talent and recruited him for the football team. *(setting scene)* Now imagine you are at the football field at the Carlisle Indian School. *(motions SL)* Here comes Pop Warner and his assistant coach.

(Enter Pop Warner SL carrying a football. He stops SC.)

Warner: Bill, I want you to see this new boy we recruited. *(calls off SR)* Thorpe! Jim Thorpe, come over here!

Jim: *(running on wearing football helmet)* Yes, Sir!

Warner: I have a little test for you. *(points off SL)* As you can see, I have positioned eleven men out on the field to represent the opposing team.

Jim: *(looking off SL)* Yes, I can see them staggered from the *(points SL)* 50 yard line over to the goal line *(points DSL)*.

Warner: Exactly! Now take this ball *(hands ball to Jim)*, stand on that goal line *(points USL)*, and run through these men to that goal line *(points DSL)*.

Jim: Yes, Sir! *(runs off USL)*

Bill: Some test! You have the first string out there. *(points)* That kid will get slaughtered before he gets to the 20 yard line!

Warner: The first string needs some tackling practice! *(shouting off SL)* Start the play!

(Both look off SL and move heads to DSL as Bill calls the action. Bill jumps up and down as though he is Jim avoiding being tackled.)

Bill: My gosh, he sidestepped the end *(sidesteps)*, ducked the guard *(ducks)*, spun around the tackle *(spins)*. . .

Warner: *(yelling off SL)* Tackle him, Lightfoot! Tackle him!

Bill: Zig-zagged the center *(zig-zags)*, jumped the fullback *(jumps)*, and he's free! Free for the goal! *(jumping up and down)* Touchdown! Touchdown!

Warner: Well, I'll be!

Jim: *(runs back to Warner, out of breath)* How was that, Coach?

Warner: Hey, this was supposed to be a tackling practice!

Jim: *(walking off SR)* Nobody tackles Jim Thorpe!

Bill: *(poking Warner with his elbow)* You can say that again!

Warner: I think we have a winner!

(Both exit SR.)

Wheeler: *(to the committee)* By 1908, Jim was headed for a career in football when his father died. He seemed to lose interest in school after that.

(Jim and two friends, George and Jesse, walk on SR and stand SC.)

Jim: I don't think I'm coming back to school in September.

Jesse: What are you going to do?

Jim: I honestly don't know. I just don't seem to care about school anymore.

George: Come with us. We're going to play baseball for the summer.

Jim: Baseball!

Jesse: Sure—you'll do great! I've seen you play!

George: We're playing in the Carolina League. It's a semi-professional team.

Jesse: You'll make about $15 a week.

Jim: Why not? I don't have anything else to do!

George: Great! Let's all go sign up!

(Jim, George and Jesse exit SR.)

Wheeler: And Jim Thorpe signed to play baseball in the Carolina League. In fact, Pop Warner was known to encourage some of his athletes to play summer baseball. What Jim didn't know was that other athletes signed up under false names. Jim Thorpe used his real name!

IOC Member #1: You mean other Olympic athletes of that day may have been paid for playing a sport?

Wheeler: Yes!

IOC Member #2: Why wasn't it brought to light?

Wheeler: It was common practice. Coaches encouraged it. And the athletes only made 2 or 3 dollars a game!

Samaranch: I see. Please go on.

Wheeler: Well, Jim soon tired of just "kicking" around the country, and when he finally got back to Oklahoma, there was a letter from Pop Warner urging him to return to school.

IOC Member #3: Did he return?

Wheeler: He sure did. He was on the train the next day heading for Carlisle. And what a season it was!

(Jim enters SR wearing football helmet and a football tucked under his arm.)

Wheeler: Jim passed *(Jim fakes a throw)*, kicked *(Jim fakes kick)*, blocked *(Jim leans into block position)* and ran! *(Jim runs across from SR to SL.)* Listen to this. *(Wheeler picks up paper off of desk and reads)* "Carlisle Indian School led by Jim Thorpe beat *(Jim walks across from SL to SR, casually tossing ball in air)* Yale, Pittsburgh, Chicago and all other big college teams including Army!" *(Jim drops on knee in football pose of the early 1900's.)* In fact, in the Army game, Jim caught a kick on the 10 yard line and ran *(Jim picks up ball, rises and runs across stage and off SL)* 90 yards to a touchdown. The referee declared him offside. *(walks to R side of table and talks to IOC member sitting there)* Now listen to this. You want to know what kind of man Jim Thorpe was? *(IOC Member nods "yes.")* Well, Jim came back to where he started *(Jim returns to SR)*, received the kick again and ran *ninety-five* yards to a touchdown. That year he was named All-American halfback! Five big-league baseball teams were trying to sign him up.

Samaranch: What about the 1912 Olympics?

Wheeler: That started out as a near disaster. Picture the locker room at the stadium in Stockholm. *(crosses SL and reaches off SL for two pairs of shoes and brings them and an empty chair DSC)* Pop Warner was Coach of the American Olympic Track Team.

(Jim enters from SL, barefoot, and starts looking under chair for his shoes. Pop Warner runs on from SL.)

　　　　More Short Plays for the Classroom—Intermediate　　　　No. 2479

Warner: *(excited)* The officials have called for starters for the 200-meter race.

Jim: *(looking under chair again)* I can't find my shoes!

Warner: You don't have your spikes? You've got less than a minute to get out there.

Jim: Never mind, Pop. *(picks up a pair of shoes from the floor and tries them on.)* I'll wear these old ones! Someone must have thrown them away! *(runs off SL)*

Voice off SL: Take your places!

(gun fires and crowd cheers)

Warner: *(sits on chair depressed)* My star runner in cast-off shoes. We'll never win a medal.

Voice off SL: The winner in 22.9 seconds is . . . Jim Thorpe of the United States!

Warner: I don't belive my ears! *(rises and walks off SL in a daze)* What'll he do when he finds his shoes??

Wheeler: *(to IOC)* You all know his Olympic record.

IOC Member #1: A gold medal in the Pentathlon . . .

IOC Member #2: A gold medal in the Decathlon . . .

IOC Member #3: More points scored by him alone than the entire squads of many countries!

IOC Member #4: Voted "best athlete of the first half of the century" by the Associated Press Poll.

Secretary: *(rising spontaneously)* The King of Sweden was right! He is the greatest athlete in the world!!

(All the men turn and look at the secretary. She blushes and sits, picking up her steno pad and pencil.)

Secretary: I beg your pardon!

Samaranch: *(to Wheeler)* Go on.

Wheeler: His rocket-like career came to a crashing halt when an obscure reporter scratching for news on Jim Thorpe . . .

(Reporter in a hat with "Press" card in back races on from SR and pretends to dial a telephone DSL.)

Reporter: *(talking on telephone)* Listen, Chief, stop the presses! I'm in North Carolina. Listen carefully. . .Jim Thorpe was paid to play baseball back in 1909! *(listens on telephone)* Sure! He was a professional when he participated in the Olympics in Stockholm. *(listens some more)* You're right. He'll probably lose his medals! Get it in the next edition and spell my name right for the by-line *(hangs up and runs off SR)*.

Samaranch: Then what happened?

Wheeler: Well, the president of the Amateur Athletic Association met with Jim.

(The AAU president enters SR and Jim enters SL. They meet DSC. Jim is wearing his medals and the AAU president carries a pencil and notebook.)

AAU President: *(writing in book)* You were paid to play baseball in 1909?

Jim: Yes, Sir. Two dollars a game.

AAU President: Why did you jeopardize your amateur standing?

Jim: I guess I didn't think the whole thing through carefully.

AAU President: The AAU finds you a professional! I will present our decision to Avery Brundage, President of the International Olympic Committee. *(turns and walks DSR to Brundage, who has just entered from SR)*. Mr. Brundage, the AAU finds Jim Thorpe was a professional when he performed in the 1912 Olympics! *(hands him notebook)*

Bundage: *(takes notebook, opens and reads)* We of the IOC are in agreement. Ignorance of the rules is no excuse! *(crosses up to Jim)* Jim Thorpe, our decision is that you competed at the 1912 Olympics in Stockholm as a professional. You must return your medals and your name will be stricken from the records!

Wheeler: *(crosses to end of table SR)* And Jim gave back his medals. . . *(Jim takes off medals and hands them over to Brundage, who turns and exits SR.)* . . .and then went on to achieve fame for the next 16 years as a professional athlete, retiring in 1929 at the age of 41. *(Jim exits SL.)*

IOC Member #1: Didn't he help organize the American Professional Football League?

Wheeler: Yes. You know it today as the NFL. *(crosses back SL to his chair)* Oh yes, one last thing. The AAU reversed their decision that Jim Thorpe was a professional. They sent notice to Avery Brundage that they considered Jim to be an amateur at the 1912 Olympics. *(sits)* Gentlemen, I rest my case!

Samaranch: *(standing)* We will now vote as to whether Jim Thorpe's name should be put back in the Olympic record book as Champion. *(hands out paper ballots)* Also, should we return the gold medals to his family? *(walks into audience)* You are all part of this moment in American history. *(hands out ballots to audience)* Let's all vote! We await your decision.

(The play ends when the votes are tabulated and Samaranch announces the results.)

(Actors can enter and bow.)

THE END

THE GOLD MEDALS

PRODUCTION NOTES

Use this sheet to keep personal notes about any aspect of your production: costumes, characters, stage directions, props, rehearsals, performances, evaluations, etc.

FIFTH RING OF SATURN

GETTING READY FOR YOUR PLAY

Characters:
Ben, Joe, L2, Z4, Q3, V5,
various Asteroid People.

Props:
three game cubicles,
paper balls

Suggestions: 1. Video game cubicles with tissue paper screens and joystick levers can be made from refrigerator boxes staggered on stage to keep audience from seeing Video People.
2. If unable to acquire 3 boxes, place a person inside the one box to stick hand through tissue-paper screen, withdraw hand, but remain in box while other Video People walk on.
3. Video people should wear white gloves.

CAST

Character:	Actor/Actress
Ben	_____
Joe	_____
L2	_____
Z4	_____
Q3	_____
V5	_____
Various Asteroid People	_____
	_____
	_____
	_____
	_____

FIFTH RING OF SATURN

(Scene takes place at a video arcade. Ben is watching his friend, Joe, play a video game. The screen of the video machine faces SR, putting Joe in profile. The other machines in the arcade all face SR. Joe is playing "Secret of the Fifth Ring of Saturn," and putting much "body language" into his playing. When he does well, he cheers and when he does poorly, he groans. There is much electronic beeping throughout this part of the scene. Finally...)

Ben: Come on, Joe. We've been here four hours! Your hand is going to melt into that joystick.

Joe: *(trance-like)* Yeah, you might say we're like "one."

Ben: *(tugging on Joe's free arm)* Come on, Joe. I'm really going to get it! I'm an hour late for supper already!

Joe: I can't stop now! I almost have the secret of the Fifth Ring of Saturn!

Ben: Who cares? I'm so late, my mom is going to react like an atomic explosion!

Joe: *(still playing)* Sh-h-h! I almost know the secret!

Ben: *(looking around)* Oh, my gosh! Everyone has left! We're the only ones here!

Joe: Ben, I'm winning! I'm winning!

(Beeping gets louder and lights start to flash.)

Ben: *(turns to go)* I'm going to call my mom.

Joe: *(doesn't hear him)* The secret...the secret...is...

(All noise and lights stop as a gloved hand breaks through the [tissue-paper] video screen.)

Z4: *(heard from behind screen)* Switch off, Alien! You know too much!

Joe: *(stares at screen, mouth open in amazement)* Wha-a-a-t?

(Ben and Joe stand mesmerized as four Video People walk around from the back of the video machine, all pointing gloved hands at the two boys.)

L2: *(to Joe)* Do you know the penalty for interfering with the molecular structure of the galaxy?

Joe: I'm just playing a game!

Z4: You call unbalancing the universe a *game*?

More Short Plays for the Classroom—Intermediate No. 2479

Ben: *(slowly backing off SR)* See ya, Joe. I've got to get home, ya know...Late for supper!

Q3: *(pointing to Ben)* Freeze, Alien! Unless you want to arrive at your destination as an atomic jig-saw puzzle!

Ben: No, Sir...I mean, yes, Sir...I mean..Boy, my mom is a flop at putting together a jig-saw puzzle!

L2: *(to Z4)* What shall we do with the Aliens?

Z4: This is a matter for the ruler of the Third Circuit. Put them in semi-freeze frame and they won't be able to escape.

(L2 points finger at Joe and Ben.)

Joe: *(scared)* What are you going to do?

L2: You won't feel a thing. *(wiggles finger at Ben and Joe)* Zap!

(Ben and Joe stiffen.)

V5: March!

(Ben and Joe start to walk in slow motion in a circle, picking their knees up high.)

Ben: *(to Joe)* Do you feel like you're running, Joe?

Joe: Yeah, about sixty miles an hour! But I'm not getting anywhere!

Ben: I hope my mother isn't waiting supper!

Joe: How can you think of food at a time like this?

Q3: Silence! Move faster! We have to loop into the Third Circuit before the Fifth Ring changes orbit.

(Boys pick knees up higher, but don't move in the circle any faster.)

Ben: *(whispering to Joe)* What's he talking about?

Joe: You've got me!

(Disruptive video static noises are getting louder and louder.)

Z4: We're too late! Our timing is off! The Memory Portal is closing!

L2: You're right! *(looks around in panic)* The Orbit is changing!

(All Video People move around in confusion while Ben and Joe still do slow-motion walk.)

More Short Plays for the Classroom—Intermediate   No. 2479

V5: *(running around)* The Asteroid People can attack!

Q3: We'll be bombarded!

Joe: How do they attack?

Z4: Once they penetrate the orbit of the Fifth Ring...

L2: ...they have learned to congeal the substance of the Ring...

V5: ...and bombard us with the very atmosphere in which we live!

Q3: *(looking off SL at video machines)* Here they come! We're under attack!

(Loud video static noises as Asteroid People run on throwing white paper balls. L2, V5, Z4 and Q3 run around in confusion ducking balls. Ben and Joe are still making a circle in slow motion.)

Z4: *(sinks to knees, being hit with balls)* We're doomed!

L2: *(falling on floor)* The Asteroids are winning! I can't take much more!

Ben: Unfreeze us and we'll help fight back!

Joe: We won't escape. We promise!

Z4: *(to Q3)* Release them, Q3!

Q3: *(points finger at Ben and then Joe)* Paz! Paz!

(Ben and Joe shake their arms and legs.)

Ben: Come on, Joe, it's every man for himself! *(picks up ball from ground and throws at an Asteroid Person)* Take that!

Joe: *(picking up a ball and throwing)*...and that! *(picks up more balls to throw)*

V5: *(picks up ball and throws)* ...and that!

Ben: *(to Video People)* Now you're talking. Fight back! We can win!

(Ben, Joe, and Video People drive the Asteroid People off SL behind the video machines, throwing all the balls off stage L.)

Ben: *(holding the last ball in his hand and inspecting)* You know, Joe, this looks like a popcorn ball. *(tastes it)* Yeah, it's a popcorn ball!

Joe: A what?

V5: *(walking to video machine and peering into screen)* The Memory Portal is starting to open!

Z4: It's a miracle! We can slip back into the Fifth Ring and avoid the 3rd Circuit!

Q3: But, we have only seconds!

L2: And we need guidance—expert guidance!

Joe: We'll guide you back! *(to Ben)* Won't we, Ben?

Ben: We will?

Z4: But, you have gained your freedom!

V5: You may be trapped forever in this Asteroid Belt!

Joe: Don't waste time talking! *(moves to video machine and puts hand on joystick)* We'll take our chances, won't we Ben?

Ben: We will?

(Video People slowly back off SL behind machine and start to make beeping noises.)

Z4: *(backing off)* You're a hero!

L2: *(backing off)* We are eternally grateful!

Q3: *(backing off)* Now you know the secret of the Fifth Ring of Saturn.

V5: It is made of popcorn.

(All Video People make beeping noises as they disappear behind video machine.)

Joe: *(in a trance in front of video machine)* The secret is . . . the secret is . . . popcorn! POPCORN? *(coming out of trance)* What a dumb game! The secret of the Fifth Ring of Saturn is, it is made of popcorn!

Ben: *(tossing ball)* That makes sense.

Joe: *(turning to Ben)* It does? *(looks at ball)* Where did you get that popcorn ball?

More Short Plays for the Classroom—Intermediate No. 2479

Ben: You don't remember?

 Joe: No, I was really into that dumb game. The last thing I remember is you were going to call your mom. What did she say?

Ben: Oh...well...The line was busy! Ah...while I was telephoning I...ah...got hungry and bought some popcorn.

 Joe: Boy, you're always hungry. Come on, let's go home. You can telephone her and tell her you'll have dinner at my house. *(starts to leave SR)*

Ben: That's good, 'cause my mother would never believe why I'm late! *(starts to leave SR with Joe)*

 Joe: *(looking back at video machine)* Popcorn! What a dumb game! *(exits SR)*

Ben: *(starting to eat popcorn)* You said it! *(exits SR)*

THE END

FIFTH RING OF SATURN

PRODUCTION NOTES

Use this sheet to keep personal notes about any aspect of your production: costumes, characters, stage directions, props, rehearsals, performances, evaluations, etc.

THE VISIT

GETTING READY FOR YOUR PLAY

Characters:
Debbie, Carla, Sandra, Jean, Tim,
Mark, John, Edison, Bob,
Various Chums of Tom Alva,
Tom Alva Edison (as a boy),
Tom's Mother, Peter

Props:
school books, telephone, table,
8 chairs, lamp, telephone book,
record player, 5 record albums,
TV, newspapers, box to sell
candy and peanuts, bucket of
type, bowl of popcorn, money to
buy newspapers, candy, peanuts

Suggestions:
1. Passengers on train can put on old-fashioned hats to set feeling for the era.
2. Wrap belts around school books to carry them in the style of the day.
3. Place shoulder straps on box for selling papers, candy and peanuts.
4. TV does not have to function as audience sees only the back.
5. Choose five record album titles for scene on page two.

CAST

Character:	Actor/Actress
Debbie	_____
Carla	_____
Sandra	_____
Jean	_____
Tim	_____
Mark	_____
John	_____
Edison	_____
Bob	_____
Various Chums of Tom Alva	_____
	_____
	_____
	_____
Tom Edison (boy)	_____
Tom's Mother	_____
Peter	_____

THE VISIT

(Scene takes place in the family room of Debbie's house on a Saturday afternoon. Three girls are sitting around a table talking. Enter Debbie...)

Debbie: Mom says we can invite the boys over and dance.

Everyone: *(ad-libbing)* Great! Super! Oh boy! etc. etc.

Debbie: And she says we can make popcorn!

Carla: *(reaches for telephone)* Let's call them. They're only two doors away at Tim's house. Do you have his number?

Debbie: *(pointing)* It's in that book, next to the telephone.

Carla: *(squinting, looking through book)* Sandra, could you turn on the light, please. It's getting dark in here! *(points SL)* The switch is over there.

Sandra: *(walks SL and pretends to switch on light)* How's that?

Carla: Better! *(looks in book)* Here it is! *(dials telephone and waits)* Tim?... Hi, it's Carla. We're at Debbie's. Can you guys come over and dance?... Well, we're going to have popcorn...

Debbie: *(afraid they might not come over)* And ice cream!

Carla: And ice cream!... *(waits listening—then smiles)* Good!

Jean: Have him bring his portable record player.

Carla: And can you bring your record player? *(pause)* Good! See you soon!

Sandra: *(looking at TV placed with back toward audience)* Look at this old silent movie!

(Melodrama music plays as Debbie, Carla and Jean walk over to look.)

Jean: Gosh, aren't movies funny when you can't hear people talk?

Sandra: I like it better when you can hear the words. I wonder who invented sound for movies?

Debbie: I don't know! Come on, let's move these chairs back so we can dance! *(Everyone moves furniture as doorbell rings.)*

Carla: There they are!

Debbie: I'll let them in! *(exits SL)*

(Girls continue to arrange furniture. Enter boys SL. Everyone exchanges "hi's" and "hello's".)

Tim: Here's the record player. (*places on table*)

Mark: . . . And here are some records. (*hands Sandra five albums*)

Sandra: (*looks through the albums and names each one out loud*)
———, ———, ———, ———, ——— These are great!

John: Let's put one on and dance. (*John puts on record and everyone dances.*)

(*Doorbell rings, but no one hears it because music is loud. An old man [(Edison)] appears at the door to the room SL. Everyone stops dancing. Debbie stops the record.*)

Debbie: Who are you?

Edison: I rang the bell. Don't you folks have it hooked up to electricity?

Carla: Who . . . who . . . are you?

Edison: Some people just don't have faith in electricity! Let me tell you—it works!

Bob: (*amazed*) Who *are* you?

Edison: (*taking off hat and bowing*) Forgive me. I'm Thomas Alva Edison.

John: Thomas Edison!

Tim: *The* Thomas Edison in the school books?

Sandra: You're—dead!

Edison: Most of the time—but on my birthday I like to visit people.

Debbie: February 11th is your birthday?

Edison: Yes, it is. I'm one hundred-and thirty years old!*

Bob: (*sits*) I don't believe this is happening!

(*Others sit in disbelief.*)

Edison: You'll get used to it. The others always have. (*walks around and looks*) Well, you *do* believe in electricity. You're using quite a few of my inventions.

Everyone: We are?

Edison: Sure! (*points*) The phonograph, the sound for movies . . .

* *Note: Edison was born in 1847. You may update his "age" accordingly.*

Sandra: Really?

Edison: . . .the telephone transmitter (*lifts the telephone*), plus the electric train, plus the stock market ticker, et cetera, et cetera, et cetera, and . . .(*walks SR to switch and turns it off*)

Mark: Hey, it's dark in here! (*Everyone jumps up and ad libs about darkness.*)

Edison: (*switches on the switch*) The incandescent light!

John: You invented all that? You must have gone to college forever to learn all that!

Edison: Well, that's another story. Do you have time?

(*Everyone sits*)

Debbie: (*sitting*) All the time in the world.

Edison: (*backing US*) I'm going to take you back to 1858, when I was eleven. . .
(*Enter young Thomas Edison and a group of school chums.*)

Chums: (*singing*) Tom is a dummy. . .Tom is a dummy. . .Tom is a dummy. . . (*exit SR leaving young Edison SC crying*)

Mother: (*entering*) Al, why are you standing out here in front of the house crying?

Tom Alva: The kids say I'm dumb because I ask impossible questions! Teacher thinks I am too!

Mother: What questions do you ask?

Tom Alva: Well. . .(*thinks*) "How do birds fly?" and "Why are rocks hard?" and "Why does water run downhill?"

Mother: That does it! You are going to stay home and *I'll* teach you. I guess the teacher is too busy to answer your questions.

(*Both exit SR.*)

Edison: (*walking around table telling his story*) And I stayed home and studied. By the time I was twelve I had read seven volumes of a history of England and five volumes of a history of the world.

Everyone: (*ad libbing*) Gee!. . .Wow!. . .You read that?. . .etc. etc.

Edison: And since I was interested in physics, I was busy conducting experiments in my laboratory down in the basement...until one day I added two potent powders...(*pretends he is pouring something*) and...KAARRROOOOMMMMM!!!

Tim: What happened?

(*Mother enters SL, takes a few steps, and shouts down into an imaginary basement.*)

Mother: (*shouting*) Al, I know you're a curious boy, but you are going to have to move your laboratory out of the basement! Your father's soup fell off the table into his lap! (*exit SL*)

Carla: What did you do after that?

Edison: Well, I got my first job as a train boy.

Bob: But you were only twelve!

Edison: Oh, that was nothing! In 1859 a lot of twelve-year-old boys were supporting their families or running away to sea. (*thinking back*) Besides, I was quite an *entrepreneur*!

John: What's an "entre—"..."entre—"...?

Edison: Here, I'll show you. Put the chairs in line like seats in a train coach and sit on them...

(*The four girls and four boys arrange chairs parallel to audience facing SR with aisle and sit.*)

Edison: Now you'll be train passengers. (*While passengers are setting scene, Edison continues to talk.*)

Edison: Imagine it is 1859, and the Grand Trunk Railroad Company has decided to lay tracks from Port Huron, Michigan, where I live, to Detroit, fifty miles away. I heard they needed a train boy...

(*Enter young Tom SR selling papers and candy and walking down aisle the length of chairs.*)

Tom: Peanuts! Candy! Get your newspapers here! Magazines! Candy!...

Carla: (*pretending to be a passenger*) Here, boy! I'll take a newspaper! You're pretty young to be going to Detroit!

Sandra: (*pretending to be a passenger*) Since there is only one train, you'll have to spend eight hours in Detroit before the train returns!

Bob: *(as passenger)* Yes, how do you spend your time in the big city, young man?

Tom: I go to the Detroit Free Library.

Mark: The library?

Tom Alva: Yep! I plan to read a foot *(holds hands a foot apart)* of books a week!

Debbie: *(as passenger)* Land sakes, young man, you just might amount to something if you keep doing all that reading.

Tom Alva: *(smiling)* Yes, Ma'am. *(exits waving newspaper)* Newspapers! Candy! Peanuts!

Edison: *(sitting on train talking to "passengers")* By 1860, they added an express train, and I bought fruits and vegetables in Detroit, opened two stores in Port Huron and hired three boys—two to run the stores and one to sell the food on the express train. I was 13 years old—and that, my young man, *(to John)* is an "entrepreneur!"

John: Wow!

Edison: *(rising)* And that isn't all! It is the year 1861, the start of the Civil War. People wanted news of the war. *(turns to Mark)* Didn't have radios in those days! *(pulls Mark and a chair DSC)* You are the telegraph operator *(seats Mark, who looks blank)* You know...dit dit dit...dah dah dah...dit dit dit.

(pretends he is working a telegraph key)

Mark: *(gets into play acting)* Oh, yeah! *(taps with fingers on pretend telegraph key)* I'm sending a message!

(Edison nods approval.)

Edison: *(pulls Peter DSR with chair)* And you are a printer. *(seats him, reaches off DSR, and sets bucket of type by chair on floor.)* Print!

Peter: *(pretends to operate printing press)* Yes, Sir!

Edison: *(pulls Debbie, Jean, Tim and John DSR)* And you are Detroit passengers waiting for the train from Port Huron. *(Passengers ad-lib among themselves.)*

Tom Alva: *(enters and goes DSR to talk to printer)* I'm Tom Edison. Could I buy that bucket of type and that old printing press?

Peter: Sure. Do you know how to set type?

Tom Alva: No, but I'm willing to learn!

Peter: With spirit like that, I'll teach you for nothing! *(pretends to teach Tom)*

Edison: *(walks DSR and puts his hand on young Tom's shoulder)* And I learned to set type and *(picks up bucket, accidentally spilling some type on floor)* started printing a newspaper in the baggage car of the train. *(Both walk USC to chairs and young Tom pretends to hand print.)* Then I went to my friend, the telegraph operator at the train station in New Haven.

Tom Alva: *(walking DSC)* Hey, Sam, can you get me the latest war news over your telegraph?

Jim: Sure! *(starts to work telegraph and write information on papers)* What do you want this for?

Tom Alva: I'm starting a newspaper and the people in Detroit want their news hot off the press! *(takes imaginary paper, walks USL, and pretends to set type and print)*

Edison: And that's what they got from my newspaper, *The Weekly Herald*—along with a little local gossip, of course. *(chuckles)*

Tom Alva: *(walking length of chairs holding up imaginary newspaper)* Get your latest news here in the *Weekly Herald!*

Sandra: *(as passenger)* I'll take one, Tom. Incidentally, Mrs. Foster over in Mount Clemens had triplets yesterday!

Tom Alva: Thanks, Mrs. Bennet. You'll see the story in next week's paper!

Edison: And sometimes the people in Detroit were so anxious to get the news of the war, they would pay triple!

Tom Alva: *(walking by Detroit passengers)* Get the latest news of the war!

Debbie: *(shouting)* Over here! I'll pay ten cents!

Jean: I want one! I want one! I'll pay a quarter!

Tim: *(shouting)* Over here! Over here! Here's fifty cents—keep the change!

John: What's the latest on the war? Name your price!

Edison: (*moving a passenger chair to original place in room*) Well, that's how it all started!

(*Everyone arranges chairs into original positions while talking. All sit when chairs are in place.*)

Debbie: How many things did you invent?

Edison: Well, as far as I can recall, I invented over a thousand different things!

Tim: That's amazing!!

Edison: My motto is "Find out what the world needs and then go ahead and try to invent it."

Jean: How did you find the time?

Edison: That was no problem. I worked an average of 20 hours a day. When I was tired, I "catnapped" for about a half hour and always woke up refreshed!

John: Was it easy to invent things?

Edison: That depended on what is was. The phonograph was a snap! (*snaps fingers*) But other things required hundreds of experiments.

Carla: Did you ever quit?

Edison: No, it's my nature to persist. There was no such thing as failure in my life. I learned by my mistakes. For instance, I worked for thousands of hours on my greatest invention, the incandescent light bulb, until I finally found the correct filament. (*thinking back*) October 21, 1879. I'll never forget!

Tim: It's hard to imagine what it was like before the electric light bulb.

Edison: (*crosses SL to switch*) Here, I'll turn off the light so you get the feeling of why I worked so hard at it. (*pretends to turn off switch*) There!

(*When Edison says, "there," everyone closes eyes. Edison quietly leaves SL. Everyone is sitting with eyes closed as Debbie's mother enters USC and looks around.*)

Mother: (*crosses SL to lightswitch and turns it on*) What are you kids doing sitting here in the dark?

(*Everyone opens eyes and looks around.*)

Debbie: Oh, Mom, we were talking to Mr. Edison. I want you to meet. . .(*turns around*) Where is he?

(*Everyone looks and ad-libs.*)

Mother: Oh, I see. It's a new type of charades. Well, have fun. The popcorn is almost ready! (*exits UC*)

Sandra: Do you think we imagined it?

Peter: (*crosses DSR and bends to pick up something*) Look, here is some type. (*arranges type on table as others gather around. Peter spells out loud "W-e-e-k-l-y H-e-r-a-l-d."*

Carla: The Weekly Herald! Come on, turn on that Edison (*points to record player*) invention and let's dance!

(*Jim puts on record and kids dance as Mother enters with big bowl of popcorn.*)

Mother: (*smiling*) Now, that's more like it!

(*Kids smile and keep dancing.*)

THE END

THE VISIT

PRODUCTION NOTES

Use this sheet to keep personal notes about any aspect of your production: costumes, characters, stage directions, props, rehearsals, performances, evaluations, etc.

THE SANDWICH

GETTING READY FOR YOUR PLAY

Characters:
Hamburger, Bun, Lettuce, Tomato,
Pickle, Onion.

Props: See suggestions below.

Suggestions:
1. Each actor can wear a hat, scarf, or shirt depicting the color of the food he or she represents.
2. Make costumes to suggest a pickle, onion, etc. (Place a banner across Hamburger's chest saying, "Grade A #1.") The costumes could enhance the play greatly and could be a class project.
3. Make street signs saying, "Potato Street" or "French Fry Lane."

CAST

Character:	Actor/Actress
Hamburger	_____
Bun	_____
Lettuce	_____
Tomato	_____
Pickle	_____
Onion	_____

THE SANDWICH

(Scene takes place on the sidewalk in a neighborhood called "Lunch.")

Hamburger: *(Enter Hamburger, a bully type, strutting around stage.)* Hey, this is my neighborhood. It's called "Lunch" and I run things around here. As you can see, I am a Grade A, Number 1, prime hamburger patty. I'm tops in this neighborhood. *(looks SL)* Here comes my buddy, Bun. He's always hanging around me—ha, ha! *(nods head in affirmation)* Yep, he sticks to me like glue.

Bun: *(enters SL)* Hi, Hamb'. What's cookin'?

Hamburger: Not much. *(points SL)* Who's that red-headed girl over there with Lettuce?

Bun: *(crosses toward SL and waves)* A new kid in the neighborhood. Lettuce is showing her around.

Lettuce: *(Enters SL with Tomato)* Hi, Bun. This is Tomato!

Bun: *(smiles)* Hi!

Hamburger: *(pushing Bun aside and crossing to Tomato and Lettuce)* I'm Hamburger—A VIP around here!

Lettuce: *(whispering to Tomato)* "VIP" means "very important patty!"

Tomato: *(rather formally)* Hello. *(looks around in boredom)* Have I met everyone around here?

Bun: No, you haven't met Pickle.

Tomato: Pickle! I'll bet he's a real sourpuss!

Lettuce: Not really. He has a great sense of humor.

Bun: When it gets dull around here, he really livens things up!

Hamburger: I don't need him around. He's a funny lookin' kid! He's got bumpy skin!!

Lettuce: *(to Hamburger)* Quiet! You'll hurt his feelings. Here he comes now!

Pickle: *(runs on stage and circles around kids)* Here I come! Zip! Zip! Zip!

Hamburger: *(pushes him off stage)* And there you go! Trip! Trip! Trip!!

Tomato: *(to Lettuce)* That wasn't very nice!

Lettuce: Hamburger doesn't like any competition.

Tomato: Well, I thought he was cute! *(looks around)* Have I met everyone in the neighborhood?

Bun: No, you haven't met Onion. Here he comes now! *(Enter Onion. Everyone holds their noses.)*

Onion: Hi, gang. Can I play?

Tomato: *(rubbing eyes)* You make me cry!

Hamburger: *(pushing Onion)* Get lost, kid! You stink!

Onion: *(crosses and sits on floor DSL and cries.)* Nobody likes me!

Lettuce: What will we play?

Bun: I know, let's play Sandwich!

Lettuce: *(to Tomato)* He always likes to play Sandwich because he always gets to play two parts—top bun and bottom bun.

Hamburger: OK, we'll start with me—the most important part of the sandwich. I'll tell everyone where to stand!

Lettuce: That figures!

Hamburger: Tomato, you stand next to me. *(Tomato skips around in a circle and stands left of Hamburger.)* Lettuce, you're kind of weak. You stand next to Tomato. *(Lettuce walks weakly, dragging her feet and exaggerating her weakness. She finally stands next to Tomato and then sticks out tongue at Hamburger.)* OK, Bun! Do your stuff!

Bun: *(runs to right of Hamburger)* Now I'm top bun! *(runs to left of Lettuce)* Now I'm bottom bun! *(runs to right of Hamburger)* Now I'm top bun! *(runs to left of Lettuce)* Now I'm bottom bun! *(runs to right of Hamburger)* Now I'm top bun!

Hamburger: Stop! You're getting me dizzy!

Bun: *(thinks, then walks behind group—one hand on Hamburger's shoulder and one hand on Lettuce's shoulder)* There, how's that? I'm an open-faced sandwich!

Hamburger: Much better.

(They all stand there—blank faces—staring at audience.)

Tomato: Something's missing!

Lettuce: This is the most nothing sandwich I've ever been in.

More Short Plays for the Classroom—Intermediate   No. 2479

Bun: I'm going to call Pickle. *(He lets go of shoulders and crosses SR. Lettuce, Tomato and Hamburger start to wiggle and droop. Bun looks back, sees sandwich start to fall apart and calls offstage in desperation.)* Pickle! Pickle! Get in here, quickly! This sandwich needs some support!

Pickle: *(runs on)* I'm here! I'm here! *(runs around sandwich)* Zip, zip!! *(crowds close to Hamburger on right side)*

Hamburger: *(poking Pickle with elbow)* Not too close, kid!

(They all stand there—blank faces—staring at audience.)

Tomato: Something is still missing!

(Onion sniffles from the corner. All heads turn and look at him.)

Bun: That's it! We need Onion! *(walks over to Onion and reaches down to help him up)* Hey, buddy, we need you!

Tomato: *(crosses over to help)* Yes, this sandwich is nothing without you! You'll give us a lift!

Pickle: Come, stand next to me! *(Everyone is back in their places, but starting to droop as Onion gets in line.)*

Onion: *(standing up tall)* Do I really give you a lift? *(Everyone takes a deep breath and stands up tall—eyes wide open.)*

Lettuce: You said it!

Hamburger: You're right. If you take the time to know a person, they can really surprise you!

Bun: *(standing behind—arms stretched around everyone)* This is the best sandwich ever!

(Everyone smiles and bows.)

THE END

THE SANDWICH

PRODUCTION NOTES

Use this sheet to keep personal notes about any aspect of your production: costumes, characters, stage directions, props, rehearsals, performances, evaluations, etc.